For As It Is The Mind That Makes The Body Rich

Also by Torry Fountinhead

The 7 Pillars Your Authentic Self Stands On, Part I of *The Essential Companion Series*

The Beauty, Part I of *The Contemplation Series*

The Soul's Openner, Part II of *The Contemplation Series*

Reach The Fountain Of Youth, Part III of *The Contemplation Series*

Shush! It's a Secret, The Lake Hides His Dummy, Part of *The Rainbow of Life's Secrets*

Poem: Good Enough, Part of *Forever Spoken, The International Library of Poetry*

A Tip of an Iceberg Meditations, a series of short books among are:

Is Forgiving a Riddle?

Momentary Thoughts

The Life The Heart Sprouts

For As It Is The Mind That Makes The Body Rich

and many more at work...

For As It Is The Mind That Makes The Body Rich

Part IV of "A Tip of an Iceberg Meditations" Series

By

Torry Fountinhead

Airé Libré Publishing & Computing Ltd.

eBook ISBNs:
ISBN-10: 0-9733450-7-1
ISBN-13: 978-0- 9733450-7-0
Print Book ISBNs:
ISBN-10: 0-9733450-9-8
ISBN-13: 978-0-9733450-9-4

© 2018 Torry Fountinhead
All Rights of this work are Reserved. No part or whole may be used, copied or reproduced, stored in retrieval systems, or transmitted, in any form or by any means whatsoever, including electronic media, mechanical, photocopying, recording, or otherwise.
For more information contact:
Airé Libré Publishing & Computing Ltd.
Suite 306, 185-911 Yates St.
Victoria BC V8V 4Y9 Canada
Tel: 1-250-592-3099.
http://www.al.bc.ca   info@al.bc.ca

Book Web-Site URLs:
http://formindbody.atipofanicebergmeditations.ca

Part of:
Http://www.atipofanicebergmeditations.ca
Http://www.tipofaniceberg.ca
Http://www.atipofanicebergmeditations.com
Http://www.tipofaniceberg.com

"For 'tis the mind that makes the body rich; And as the sun breaks through the darkest clouds,
So honour peereth in the meanest habit. What is the jay more precious than the lark,
Because his fathers are more beautiful?"

William Shakespeare
"Taming of the Shrew"

Table of Content

For As It Is The Mind That Makes The Body Rich i

For As It Is The Mind That Makes The Body Rich iii

Table of Content v

For As It Is The Mind That Makes The Body Rich vii

    Prologue 1

    I 5

    II 11

    III 15

    IV 19

    V 23

    VI 27

    VII 31

    III 35

    IX 39

    X 43

    Epilogue 45

    A word about this series 49

For As It Is The Mind That Makes The Body Rich

For As It Is The Mind That Makes The Body Rich

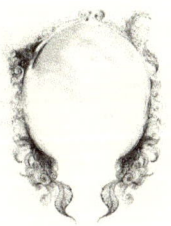

Prologue

What would it have been, if not for our minds?

The Mind – our creative abilities are affected by it, and our mind-set is the indicator of where we are.

Our consciousness's tool is our mind, so how important is it, what we hold in it?

Our minds are that part of us that grants value, or takes it away – we are the creators of our own yardsticks – whether we invented them ourselves, or accepted them from others.

In reality, all has value, yet, sometimes our minds acknowledge it, and sometimes not.

It is in the same way that 'the beauty is in the eye of the beholder.'

We can only see with our own eyes, whether the physical ones, or our mind's eyes.

In this momentary look at things, I ponder, to a degree, the question I had throughout my life, and that arose in me yet again while, watching William Shakespeare's play *Taming of the Shrew*.

Our mind, as the tool of our consciousness, is a sit of many aspects of us. It is not only our intellect, but also our awareness, discerning power, perception power, our emotional measurer, and last but not least – the conglomerations of our beliefs, knowledge, and opinions – some container it is!

Our mind may be affected by our bodily condition, as much as it, in itself, can and may affect our bodily condition.

We may approach it, as the owners of it – like the Soul being the navigator of our life, or we may be sub-servient to its tyranny, as unfortunately, it may also contain in its vast room, our fears and anxieties.

This conglomeration creates the basis for our assumptions, and who can say that their assumptions were always right?

We can only assume if we employ some discerning power, but it can only take into consideration what we already know.

Therefore, what we hold in our minds, in any particular moment, will affect the accuracy of our assumptions, but do not despair further on there is hope.

Please indulge me while I look with you, as I might use metaphors, or analogies, from the play, as well as of my own.

For As It Is The Mind That Makes The Body Rich

For As It Is The Mind That Makes The Body Rich

I

In the past, I remember noticing, and thereafter hearing, that the most precious things in life come free to us while, the most expansive things are those that may always be replaced.

Come free?!

Meaning only – that money really cannot purchase them for you – you either have it, or not.

Sometimes, one may think that money purchased their happiness etc. for them, but it does not. These things cannot have substance given to them by money – it is only the Human Being that may induce substance to them.

Love is one such a free thing.

Honour is another such a free thing.

Respect too.

Let me make sure that you do understand that I do value the actions, efforts, and all evidences that a person will bring forth to earn love, honour, and respect, but at times – although they might be earnable, or should be acknowledged, they might not be present.

From childhood, I wondered how different people could produce different definitions as to what has value, and what has not. Yet, I believed, unlike other peoples' opinions, that surely there has to be a value that is granted from the moment of creation versus acknowledged, or not, by onlookers.

Take roses versus carnations for example. Many prefer the one to the other, but surely the beauty, smell, and endearing qualities of each of the flowers should not cause arguments. They are each full of an incredible value – and it is a matter of taste, which one you would like best.

People will express their opinion, as per their taste – there are a few that will allow for an all-encompassing loving approach, without picking favourites.

In Shakespeare's era, husbands provided their wives with shelter, clothing, food, and protection; and the wives made a home, family, and brought forth the cohesive factor that tied them all together.

The support was mutual, and thus, you would expect, the respect should be.

In that era, like today, a lot of value was put on tangible riches, and status.

Alas, love was not something that was given in abundance, as parents certainly shown preference to those children they could tolerate, or manage – as those children in turn, would become easy to carry on the line, as the parents planned it.

If one child, as it is portrayed in the play *Taming if the Shrew*, was loved better, the other landed up displaying her pains and fears in anger and outbursts in such a way that concealed her beauty, wit, greatness, and potential.

She became a shrew, for lack of being understood, and appreciated.

In an era where versatility would have been valued in other places – other than your own home, they expected a certain code of behaviour, mainly obedience. Alas, they did not necessarily given the much needed nurturing to induce it.

Furthermore, as independence was not such commonplace, the options available for the daughters were not equal to those of the sons.

Children were viewed as possessions, to further the parents' alliance and riches, and not as creations to be marvelled for their own sake.

I am quite sure that even in the centuries since past, we could find exactly the same outlook, as well as treatment towards children.

It all depends where one's aspirations are stemming from.

In *Much Ado About Nothing*, Shakespeare commented about the Bible's blessing that: "The World Should Be Peopled", so although the original aspiration was to bless Humanity with a good life on Earth, it took many turns since.

Human Being introduced the 'how'.

With the 'how', class systems, racism, favouritism, mine-is-better-than-yours arguments,

For As It Is The Mind That Makes The Body Rich

etc. etc. etc., were born to taunt us all, and our history is a large body of evidence of it.

Imagine if Humans will embrace the 'gift' of children, and love them all – how more true they may be to the original 'gift'.

One may ask, what is the mind's role?

For As It Is The Mind That Makes The Body Rich

II

The importance of the mind may be found, starting with the acknowledgement of its abilities.

After all, the mind is but one of the tools available to us to live a conscious life, and be aware.

It is interesting that Shakespeare said (within the quote as mentioned in this book's opening), ***And as the sun breaks through the darkest clouds, So honour peereth in the meanest habit.***

For us, the sun is always glorious, as for

people of all eras; and a day, in which the sun breaks through the clouds, dark or not, always uplifts our spirits, and bring a smile to both our face and heart.

Yet, Shakespeare says 'honour your peers (your equals), with the meanest habit (the simplest dress – no frills), like the sun.

When comparing the glorious sun, as is, to the shrew's simple appearance, he pays her a very high compliment – *as you are*, you are as the glorious sun – have that thought held in your mind.

This is an example to how an onlooker may be appreciative of inner greatness, rather than the superficial dress displayed.

Even if one would like to understand this sentence as, *when* the sun breaks through, we can still see that Shakespeare meant to comment on the appearance, and not the time, because he refers to the Jay versus the Lark in the next part of the quote.

It reminds me something the late Audrey Hepburn had said, as follows:

"The beauty of a woman is not in the clothes she wears, the figure that she carries, or the way she combs her hair. The beauty of a woman is seen in her eyes, because that is the doorway to her heart, the place

where love resides. True beauty in a woman is reflected in her soul. It's the caring that she lovingly gives, the passion that she shows. The beauty of a woman only grows with passing years. Let a woman you respect and care for, know you see her true beauty!"

Certainly, it seems that Audrey Hepburn had experienced this truth herself.

In order to appreciate an inner beauty, one has to be able to appreciate the value of the person. Here we come again to the idea that we either are in a mindset that recognises value, or not.

The role of our mind is to be actually the proficient tool of our consciousness, and as such, it has to let go of judgements, and criticism, and concentrate on evaluating unconditionally.

If one realises that the mind is a tool, and not the master of us, we may then put it in a true perspective.

Compare the mind to a boat whereby, you – namely, your Soul and inner self will always be the Captain and the navigator of your life. Where the rudder would be the input facilitator from the outside world, the wind behind your sails would be propelled by your aspirations and the water underneath would denote the general emotional state of life where you pass.

    The boat is your tool to journey and arrive at your destination – it is not your life. You are in charge of it, and not the opposite.

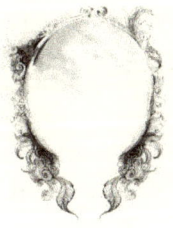

III

The Truth is clouded by the perception of it.

I would like to think that there is a Truth, (with capital T), that is 'correct' and applies to all, and then there is the personal truth of each person.

The differentiation between the two types will be initiated by the person's perception.

Every person's perception is affected by many arguments, not in the least are the belief systems held, and the conditioning accrued through life.

If one looks at the simplest example of the several colour-blindness afflictions, from seeing only a gray-scale, to red-green colour-blindness, to blue-yellow colour-blindness, and comparing it to a full colour-sight. One may see how different people will look at exactly the same item, may it be a beautiful flower, or the several coloured Canadian money notes, and develop a different perception of it.

Even without a physical impediment, if you will take ten painting artists, supply them with exactly the same paints, brushes, and canvases, and position them together in the same spot, in front of a beautiful sunset – you will get ten different sunset paintings – no two will be alike.

Ask yourself, why?

You will come to the conclusion that what is different about the people, would have had an influence on their perception of the sunset, and therefore, the outcome conveyed in the painting.

The sunset as such, is one and only. Although, the scenery is changing, ten witnesses saw it all at the same time.

All that we stand for, our gender, age, experience, knowledge, opinions, understanding, awareness level, practicality, spirituality, cultural influence and education, tastes and preferences, beliefs, and so on, affects our perception.

We do not see the same, equally.

I would like to offer a side comment here, and say that in our differences, we find the origin to our different experiences. If we were all identical, how could you differentiate us from robots?

With regards to the truth then, who is to say which one is right?

For As It Is The Mind That Makes The Body Rich

For As It Is The Mind That Makes The Body Rich

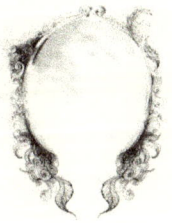

IV

Following the same idea of perception, let us compare people to fruit trees.

Humanity is like a huge orchid encompassing many types of fruit trees.

I relate to each and every person as a valuable being, who is, like a fruit tree, capable of bearing fruits that may enhance their own, and others' lives.

No person, born on this Earth, is useless –

no one!

The people you have met that seem to have not borne fruit yet, do still have the seeds inside them – it is just that they have not germinated, as yet.

Like fruit trees, so are people, in need of nourishment of many types, and from various directions. They need taking care of – lovingly.

Furthermore, no fruit tree is better than another, both in type, quality, or quantity, because it does take several things to bring forth the best in each, and then, of course, there is the question of taste.

Even in the book of Genesis, in the Bible's Old Testament, and let us assume that I may use it here at least as a good descriptive example, The Creator said that all was Good, at the end of each creational phase.

We should not humanize The Creator, but if we were to declare that our own creations, and or performances, are good – surely this will be emanating from a feeling of satisfaction.

If now we relate to the Truth again, you may see how a mind-set based on 'seeing the good' in things may influence our perception.

A dissatisfied person is a person that nothing for them may be declared enough, good, or enjoyable, as they will always reach for 'more.'

Yes, by all mean, raise the bar, but remember that each stage is to be gone through in the best way possible. One should be able to look back and say that the planning, creating, execution, and results, were as best as could be done, at the time.

We do live in a world of duality, in which every Human Being has Free Will – the power of choice that affects us all.

Therefore, it is in our own mind-set that we will determine if we are to be mainly satisfied being, or dissatisfied ones.

I mentioned before that I believe that everything has value – whether we acknowledge it, or not. Perceiving the value is like seeing the Good in things. Seeing the Good in things, leads to a life based mainly in satisfaction, versus 'not enough.'

Imagine an infant turn toddler, It is trying to stand stable, trying to walk, and yet, falls – again, and again, and again. Does it lose faith?

No! The baby is fully 'trusting'; with the inner knowing that, his eventual destiny is to walk. (I apologise to all who were, or are, born with physical shortcomings – I am talking in general here.)

In examining the baby's feeling, and outlook, you would see that a mind-set of satisfaction is predominant, even if it is just being satisfied with the fact that it tried – onward flowing within the evolution of Life.

Being satisfied, as a result of an 'expectant' mind-set, lead to a life of growth, alas, many, in the more industrial part of the world, have adopted an outlook of 'not enough', 'more is needed.'

If you compare them to the more rurally located people, who are much more depended on nature's cycles, and conditions, you would see the minute, but very important, difference that they recognise that each phase, stage, or step, is to be lived as best as possible – and be satisfied at that.

When you seed a crop, or a tree, you have to allow the seed to germinate in its own time, neither one of us may dictate our will onto the seed.

Yes, you may better the conditions for the said seed, you may even nurture it lovingly, yet, it will germinate (or not), as per its own time.

For As It Is The Mind That Makes The Body Rich

V

There is an importance in distinguishing between Mind-sets versus opinions.

Even before looking at mind-sets and opinions, one is to actually acknowledge that the power of our mind lies in the assimilation of our experiences.

We may go through life half-asleep, and hardly register our experiences, or we may choose to 'awake' and be aware of the message, each of our experiences conveys.

In reality, our experiences are 'stories'. I actually think that we might benefit from relating to these stories as 'imposters'.

What do I mean by it?

Imagine you have gone to watch a play, or a movie, and were so engrossed in the story played in front of you that you felt, as if, you are part of it.

Were you?

Emotionally, and imaginatively, maybe you 'felt' you were, but actually – you were not.

Experience you go through, likewise, is a story. Each experience has benefits, may they be the lessons we learn from them, the emotional rollercoaster they take us through, or that that they ignite in us ingenuity and problem solving ideas.

There are many repetitions of the same 'message', but in a gradual difference that re-appear in our lives, in direct relation to whether we have learnt from them, or not.

Is it not of value what Plato written in the *Dialogue Republic* that "Necessity is the mother of inventions"?

We firstly experience something; we then

turn it into one of many things – assuming we are aware.

Those people, who we call geniuses, are people who chose to be aware, awake, and engaged participators in life.

They strive on life that present them with challenges that in turn, ignite in them the necessity to solve those challenges.

The joy of invention is their answer to the hardship of the challenge.

Here we may see why their mind-set defines their behaviour, versus to their 'opinion' of what is going on. They are not interested in indulging in opinions and stories; they are interested in moving on.

For As It Is The Mind That Makes The Body Rich

For As It Is The Mind That Makes The Body Rich

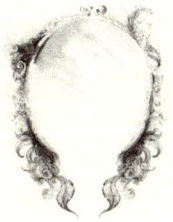

VI

Mind-set, then, becomes the foundation to our reactions, and choice making.

Now comes to my mind the song "Night and Day…"

Do not laugh, as this is exactly how Shakespeare tests our Shrew's rate of learning.

Her husband, knowing that his newly wedded wife is known to be a shrew, put her through the test of 'flowing' *with* him, versus trying to flow by *herself*. After all, they were married now, and even in that era, they looked for peace in the home, and not competition – that breeds contestation, a very unpleasant form of strife.

The husband then said that it was night while, outside, it was a broad day light. Our Shrew thought to correct him, but that led to further mean ways of deprivation, he inflicted on her.

Therefore, slowly but surely, she realised that eating and sleeping are things she cannot do without, and she started to agree with him, or at least not to contradict him.

When, as part of the test, he said it was night, so it was. When he said it was day, so it was. (a good way to have peace is not to engage in a tug-of-war!)

The content of what he said did not really matter to him, what mattered was the 'flowing with', versus not.

The differentiation was in the intention that was expressed as a mind-set. These days we have a saying 'rather be happy than be right' well, I do not really agree with it, because many a wrong acts can go uncorrected in this way, but a mind-set of co-operation versus indignation, invites understanding that may lead to an agreement.

I hope that you do realise that the play is talking about minor issues, and not moral or existential issues.

In a modern life, you may see many examples of such a situation, when you find children, for example, who get contradictory messages from their parents, only to be confused, and or become manipulative.

It reminds me of the feathers put at the end of an arrow. These feathers supposed to control the angle and direction, as well as the speed of the arrow, so if a child were like an arrow, but the parents – as feathers are pointing at opposite directions – where would the arrow go?

Clarity allows us to follow a straight line while, confusion finds us meandering here and there, arriving no-where.

Clarity may only be achieved in the home, when both parents are of the same mind-set, as well as aspire for the highest good of their children.

Look at a mind-set as a fertile soil of a certain composition. It allows you to grow only certain types of crops, and in a certain quality and quantity.

At the same time, it paints for you the 'picture' of what you are going through, using the filters of your belief systems, opinion, scars, and so on, just like filters you may use with your camera.

Our two protagonists, the shrew and her husband from the play, might have come from different backgrounds, education, tastes etc., but could make a point to have a unified-aspiration for their family and home and thus, flow together to the riches their mind can conjure.

When the mind is not encumbered by strife, it can aspire, and create a marvelous life.

You may choose to alter your mind-set to allow it to be more beneficial to you, or you may be operating in a strained fashion instead.

For As It Is The Mind That Makes The Body Rich

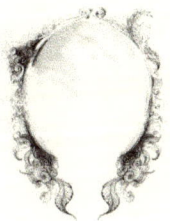

VII

Let us look at the difference between changing a mind-set versus changing an opinion.

Remember that a mind-set is directed by an intention while, an opinion by changeable things like up-to-date information, tastes, beliefs, and fashion.

It is autumn outside, and the deciduous trees' leaves are starting to turn. The gold, red, and dark red colours are taking over the lash green colour of the past spring and summer.

Your heart is open, you breathe in the scent, so special to this leaves change, and you feel that you could have become a great poet, right there.

Your mind-set is one of acknowledging the great beauty autumn brings forth, despite of the chill in the air, and the urgency to get emotionally ready for winter.

Yet, a more factual oriented person, who happens to stand by you, mentions, right at the moment when your feelings are soaring, that the reason the leaves are changing colour is because the temperature is getting colder, the tree sap ceases to flow towards the leaves – the tree, too, is getting ready for winter.

At this moment, do not change your mind-set, remain immersed in the beauty, but let go of your opinion of what should, or should not, have been said, as well as your opinion of the other person – Let Go!

You are not merged with the other person, you are an individual entitled to hold your own mind-set, and enjoy life on your own terms. Your opinions, on the other hand, could interfere with your enjoyment.

For As It Is The Mind That Makes The Body Rich

Never reduce, or diminish, a heightened mind-set, or lose the joy in it.

Besides, what good is it, if the other person does not want to be immersed in the beauty?

In the same way that we are only capable of breathing for ourselves, and not for any other person, we can discern beauty yet, not do it for another.

Our minds include within so much information, and work while comparing and associating. Each person has therefore, his or her own take on things.

The mind-set is the one that will allow you to discern while, the opinions are 'things' set previously further to comparisons, and associations.

It only takes changes in conditions etc. where you would find yourself in need of changing your opinions, but not the mind-set.

An optimist may always remain so, regardless of the changes that may take place, because they set their intention to look for the good in any situation, the lesson within, and the way to flow out of it.

Being an optimist, is a state of mind – a

mind-set.

In this era, it seems that sharing of opinions, socially, publicly, and irreverently, is in vogue, or so the existence and wide usage of social networks would attests.

Human Beings like to share both their joys, and sorrows, it is part of our makeup. There is nothing wrong with it, as we draw strength from this sharing with other caring, loving, well-wishing members of our family, and or society.

The challenge lies in the over-doing, when people lend up being engaged in the sharing of all of their emotions, awaiting acknowledgements from others, the outward looking instead for both – a balanced inward and outward looking.

The fast-paced era we live in, may also create a problem of influx of information that asks us to redefine our opinions and thus, something we put on the wall yesterday, might ridicule us today.

Being stable within our mind-set, and flowing with our opinions, renders us adaptable, gentle, and mostly independent.

VIII

In comparing communal versus personal mind-sets, we may find that there are distinct differences between opinions and mind-sets.

It is much clearer to discern between mind-sets and opinions on a community level – the larger the community, the easier it is.

Although, each will induce reactions, actions, and appearances, we should look for the intention at the base of them.

A country may choose a mind-set of tolerance versus aggression, and you will find that in the majority of that country's actions, and statement, it will be indicated so. Although, there might be some exceptions, those will come only when concrete changes advise so.

A city may be welcoming to new arrivals, or not, helping, in many ways, the people to establish themselves in it. At the same time, another city might expect you to defend for yourself.

In addition, the overall 'flavour' of the population frequency, will also set the tone of the place's mind-set.

When you find yourself going to a new country, city, community, school, and such, you will be able to 'feel' the overall atmosphere that will be effected by the mind-set, and yet, you would meet individuals who might have opinions, and behaviours, aligned with it – or not.

On a day-to-day basis, you usually meet individuals, who may, or may not, be identified with the place. Those who feel 'at home' in a place will convey its mind-set prior to adding their opinion to the mix, and those who are not, will immediately offer their opinions.

At the same time, one should take into a consideration that the overall mind-set will influence people, even prior to them forming any opinions, like children that project their own nature versus the parents' nature.

If you want to know more about a place, observe the people, and the terrain. Try to identify 'locals', and then only engage in a 'gentle' talk.

If you want to find a place that will agree with you, and will be healthy for you to be in, investigate your own mind-set, as well as the place's.

Remember, a place may change its mind-set too, but unlikely will it revert to the total opposite.

In my experience, I noticed that places have their own memory, almost, as if, that deep in the soil, memory is held like the memory held in our own muscles.

I have seen people change, both to good, or bad, when they moved to other places, and the only affect was from the actual place itself.

Even different neighbourhoods, within the same city, may behave differently.

In order not to impede our ability to evolve,

be healthy, and happy, we should look at what is good for us. We, like plant, grow in 'favourable' conditions, and not in 'challenging' ones.

We must though, investigate our own mind-sets, and opinions, and not blame a place for the limitations we set for ourselves. There are exceptions of course; I am not talking about health conditions resulting from accidents, or major events, but of general situations.

One of the neighbours, in my youth, used to say that 'every pot has the cover that will fit it', in the same way, there is a place good for each one of us. Thank Goodness, Earth is so vast.

For As It Is The Mind That Makes The Body Rich

IX

In looking at the vessel that we are, containing opinions, beliefs, tastes, and such, bearing in mind an aspiration for living the 'good life', we should strive to evolve, grow, expand, and enhance our being.

This aspiration will invite us to remain open minded, as well as open hearted.

Here we should look at what can come to our aid, from within namely, our *attitude*.

Trust begets Faith.

Faith begets Hope.

Hope allows us to be more generous in the choice of our mind-sets, and thus open us to opinions that are more congenial.

The stability that is borne of knowing ourselves deeply, will allow us to be happier within ourselves. We would look to ourselves, before looking for answers 'out there.'

We would not take part in constant critical view, neither of ourselves, nor of others.

This is not a 'Utopian' painting of reality; it is placing the responsibility right at your own feet.

You see, how can we create a home, a city, a country, a place's memory, if not by first starting it all from within?

Disregarding any of it, will only bring strife, and destruction.

Earth, nature, the plant kingdom, insects, and animals, are doing quite well without us – the Human Beings on its surface, but we affect it all.

We might be part of nature, as the physical part of us, but we are not only the physical. This is the point where the manner in which we carry our responsibility matters.

Whatever science says about our reality, it is quite obvious that a major part of the reality is a shared vision of all that occupy it. Therefore, we, who think we know so much, and are so entitled, should be more responsible.

What good is there in destruction?

None!

What good is there in growth, and collaboration?

The Good Life!

An image of a tight-rope walker comes to mind, where his ability to trust himself, and yet, measure himself, know his own reactions, keep them in-check, know when to stop and gather balance, and when to step forward.

A famous Rabbi once said that 'the whole world is a very narrow bridge, and the most important thing is not to fear at all.'

What I am trying to illustrate is that our strength comes from within. Our strength is built of number of components, not the least are trusting ourselves, because we know what we are, what skills, talents, and traits we have, not over-shooting, but remaining stable in our stance.

We also have to be cognisant of the energy we use versus the energy we spend outwardly. We do need to conserve for our own survival.

It is in our attitude that we first see if we are inclined to react, or respond. A reaction always spends our energy while, a response is a measured action that might actually be a non-action.

I certainly do not recommend creating a pent-up anger, or any other negative emotion, but as emotion is Energy in Motion, let us be wise at the manner of setting the motion on.

Exercising restriction is actually very beneficial. Being pro-active rather than re-active is also beneficial. The truth is that you would have far more control of the situation, and the outcome later on, if you keep yourself within the 'eye of the storm' – stable, other than flying all over, at the outer chaos.

In simple terms, it is wise to have both a mind-set and an attitude that strives for your highest good, and the highest good of all, it will lead you in the right direction, and to a smoother personal growth.

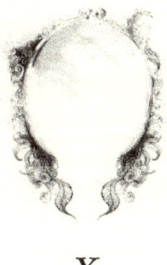

X

Last, but not least, we should remember that first impressions could become lasting impressions, and derive from our perception, both conscious, and subliminal.

If you walk into a room, and find a stifled mood, do you check to see if something has just happened? If it did not, could it be that the common denominator of all within the room is stifled?

For the same token it could be the opposite, just like New Year's Eve celebration alas, it wears off very quickly.

Going back to Shakespeare, a dress, and even a mind-set, or opinion, can give first impressions, and either proves to be 'impressive' or not.

A woman, like mentioned in the play, may wear a modest garment, but at the same time wear an outstanding dignified and confident mind-set, and will out do any fancy looking woman of no substance. Of course, it applies to men to, but the play does not relate to them in the same way.

Substance, in all subjects, stems from within. Value, both of self and other, is recognised by the inner, when a value-oriented mind-set is held firmly. Riches are within the mind.

Better, err in giving value than in making a grave mistake of dismissing it.

Even when you find that the subject does not warrants such high value, if it be a Human Being – you just granted it an uplifting aspiration, if it is of nature – trust that it has value even, if your sight is poorly, and you cannot see it, as yet.

One should not question Creation, and what is in it, we were all created with aim in mind, and who are we (as creatures) to question Creation?

For As It Is The Mind That Makes The Body Rich

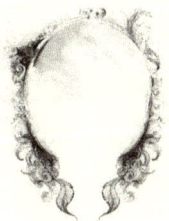

Epilogue

We conceive ideas with our minds.

We grow these ideas in the womb of our minds.

With our actions, we give them birth.

Our world would not have been what it is — if it was not so.

All that you see around you was first conceived in a mind. All that we can see was made possible because of the mind's ability to envisage, plan, and give it form.

All that was conceived in a mind – can be re-created, as the idea became already a living entity.

You can take away all the riches a person has, yet, this person will be able to recreate it, if they so inclined, as long as they are not inflicted with a major calamity. The creative secrets are in their mind.

The riches within our mind and heart enrich our lives to such an extent that we would also like them to be exhibited outwardly, in an appreciative and proud manner.

Thus, be of a valuable / valuing mind-set.

Be of Trust, and Faith.

Be of Hope.

Cherish your life, and all that is in it.

When you wish for a better life, remember to find an agreeable place for yourself. Do not judge others for where they live.

Have a mind-set that recognises that each person is worthy, decreed by Creation, therefore, let them live at their own pace, in their own way,

For As It Is The Mind That Makes The Body Rich

and if you could be of help – do not hesitate to offer it.

When Shakespeare related to us that 'it is the mind that makes the body rich', he was actually very much in line with our present day knowledge, or assumptions, of Quantum physics and mechanics.

The inkling that an idea formed in a mind capable of acknowledging it, taking it further into imagining it becoming real, can influence creation to participate, and bring it forth to a physical manifestation.

Our part is to 'simulate', creation's part is to 'operate'.

With our envisaging, as well as inducing in ourselves the feeling, as if it is already real, we make ourselves the 'midwives' of the birth of life's manifestations – for good, or the not so good.

The term 'rich' is rich in itself, as it covers multitude of things, anything from quality to quantity, vastness to deepness – it is like the ocean within that has many treasure troves, for us to discover.

Our mind is still very much a wonder, a treasure chest, and a puzzle, and this is the main reason why I only touched upon a minute part of it herein.

Life's journey is the exploration of the mind, one should engage in – and preferably, with good spirits.

No life is worthless.

All life is worthy of living, the terms may be changed using the power of your mind.

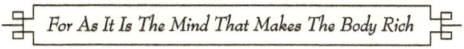

A word about this series

In this busy day and age, where people have more input than they sometimes able to concentrate on, I venture to offer a more succinct manner of dealing with subjects of interest, or need.

The image of a tip of an iceberg immediately brings to mind that there is much more unseen, underwater if you may.

Consciousness is very much like the waters of a vast sea whereby, our conscious thoughts are those that exist above the water level, and our submerged portion of the conscious – is very much our unknown part therefore, many times it is called the sub-conscious, or the un-conscious.

Our feelings are just the waves, and wave crests, which are created by the winds of time, and occurrences of life upon the surface.

I'd like to have your brief time of contemplation in reading this short book yet, to impress your mind with a profound message, and content.

It is in the succinct that we may never be overwhelmed, and in overpowering vast amount of input that we are fatigued.

I trust you know that much more could have been said about the subject of the book, but maybe what was said is enough.

I wish you joy and peace – always.

www.ingramcontent.com/pod-product-compliance
Lightning Source LLC
Chambersburg PA
CBHW020255090426
42735CB00010B/1927